SEGREGATION

BY ROBERT PENN WARREN DISCARD

"Robert Penn Warren has done an admirable and moving piece of research-writing in *Segregation*. It fills an increasingly evident void in the great amount of material published about the subject."
Ralph McGill, *The New York Times Book Review*

"The best and most understandable picture of the Deep South, caught up in a storm over desegregation."
Cleveland Press

This sympathetic, fair and honest report on seg-regation and desegregation is written by a white Southerner who recently returned to the South to find out what the whites and the Negroes want and what the future holds for both races.

In this concise book, Mr. Warren recounts his conversations with Southerners of all viewpoints, citing in their own words their attitudes on law and force, money and race, pride and resistance to change, new ambitions and old customs, emotions and equality.

MODERN LIBRARY PAPERBACKS *are published by Random House in order to make the best books of all time available to the public at a price it can readily afford.*

SEGREGATION

THE INNER CONFLICT IN THE SOUTH

ROBERT PENN WARREN

PUBLISHED BY RANDOM HOUSE
New York

Library of Congress Catalog Card Number: 57–11398

Random House IS THE PUBLISHER OF *The Modern Library*

BENNETT CERF • DONALD S. KLOPFER

Manufactured in the United States of America by H. Wolff

to Jack and Eunice

AUTHOR'S NOTE

*This report comes out of travel in Kentucky
Tennessee, Arkansas, Mississippi and Louisiana,
the parts of the South that I have known best.
It does not pretend to represent a poll-taking or
a mathematical cross section of opinion. It is a
report of conversations, some of which had been
sought out and some of which came as the result
of chance encounters.*

Part of this material has appeared in Life *magazine.*

SEGREGATION

"I'm glad it's you going," my friend, a Southerner, long resident in New York, said, "and not me." But I went back, for going back this time, like all the other times, was a necessary part of my life. I was going back to look at the landscapes and streets I had known—Kentucky, Tennessee, Arkansas, Mississippi, Louisiana—to look at the faces, to hear the voices, to hear, in fact, the voices in my own blood. A girl from Mississippi had said to me: "I feel it's all happening inside of me, every bit of it. It's all there."

I know what she meant.

To the right, the sun, cold and pale, is westering. Far off, a little yellow plane scuttles down a runway, steps awkwardly into the air, then climbs busily, learning grace. Our big plane trundles ponderously forward, feeling its weight like a fat man, hesitates, shudders with an access of sudden, building power; and with a new roar in

4

my ears, I see the ground slide past, then drop away, like a dream. I had not been aware of the instant we had lost that natural contact.

Memphis is behind me, and I cannot see it, but yonder is the river, glittering coldly, and beyond, the tree-sprigged flats of Arkansas. Still climbing, we tilt eastward now, the land pivoting away below us, the tidy toy farms, white houses, silos the size of a spool of white thread, or smaller, the stock ponds bright like little pieces of gum wrapper dropped in brown grass, but that brown grass is really trees, the toy groves with shadows precise and long in the leveling light.

Arkansas has pivoted away. It is Mississippi I now see down there, the land slipping away in the long light, and in my mind I see, idly, the ruined, gaunt, classic clay hills, with the creek bottoms throttled long since in pink sand, or the white houses of Holly Springs, some of them severe and beautiful, or Highway 61 striking south from Memphis, straight as a knife edge through the sad and baleful beauty of the Delta

5

country, south toward Vicksburg and the Federal cemeteries, toward the fantasia of Natchez.

It seems like a thousand years since I first drove that road, more than twenty-five years ago, a new concrete slab then, dizzily glittering in the August sun-blaze, driving past the rows of tenant shacks, Negro shacks set in the infinite cotton fields, and it seems like a hundred years since I last drove it, last week, in the rain, then toward sunset the sky clearing a little, but clouds solid and low on the west like a black range of mountains frilled upward with an edge of bloody gold light, quickly extinguished. Last week, I noticed that more of the shacks were ruinous, apparently abandoned. More, but not many, had an electric wire running back from the road. But when I caught a glimpse, in the dusk, of the interior of a lighted shack, I usually saw the coal-oil lamp. Most shacks were not lighted. I wondered if it was too early in the evening. Then it was early no longer. Were that many of the shacks abandoned?

Then we would pass in the dark some old

6

truck grudging and clanking down the concrete, and catch, in the split-second flick of our head-lamps, a glimpse of the black faces and the staring eyes. Or the figure, sudden in our headlight, would rise from the roadside, dark and shapeless against the soaked blackness of the cotton land: the man humping along with the croker sack on his shoulders (containing what?), the woman with a piece of sacking or paper over her head against the drizzle now, at her bosom a bundle that must be a small child, the big children following with the same slow, mud-lifting stride in the darkness. The light of the car snatches past, and I think of them behind us in the darkness, moving up the track beside the concrete, seeing another car light far yonder toward Memphis, staring at it perhaps, watching it grow, plunge at them, strike them, flick past. They will move on, at their pace. Yes, they are still here.

I see a river below us. It must be the Tennessee. I wonder on which side of us Shiloh is, and guess the right, for we must have swung far

enough north for that. I had two grandfathers
at Shiloh, that morning of April 6, 1862, young
men with the other young men in gray uniforms
stepping toward the lethal spring thickets of
dogwood and redbud, to the sound of bird song.
"One hundred and sixty men we took in the
first morning, son. Muster the next night, and
it was sixteen answered." They had fallen back
on Corinth, into Mississippi.

◀

The man in the seat beside me on the plane is
offering me a newspaper. I see the thumb of the
hand clutching the paper. The nail is nearly as
big as a quarter, split at the edges, grooved and

horny, yellowish, with irrevocable coal-black grime deep under the nail and into the cuticle. I look at the man. He is a big man, very big, bulging over the seat, bulging inside his blue serge. He is fiftyish, hair graying. His face is large and raw-looking, heavy-jowled, thick gray eyebrows over small, deep-set, appraising eyes. His name, which he tells me, sounds Russian or Polish, something ending in *-ski.*

I begin to read the paper, an article about the riots at the University of Alabama. He notices what I am reading. "Bet you thought I was from down here," he said. "From the way I talk. But I ain't. I was born and raised in New York City, but I been in the scrap business down here ten years. Didn't you think I was from down here?"

"Yes," I say, for that seems the sociable thing to say.

He twists his bulk in the blue serge and reaches and stabs a finger at the headline about Alabama. "Folks could be more gen'rous and fair-thinking," he says. "Like affable, you might say, and things would work out. If folks get affable and contig'ous, you might say, things sort of get worked out in time, but you get folks not being affable-like and stirring things up and it won't work out. Folks on both sides the question."

He asks me if I don't agree, and I say, sure, I agree. Sure, if folks were just affable-like.

I am thinking of what a taxi driver had said to me in Memphis: "Looks like the Lucy girl wouldn't want to go no place where people throwed eggs at her and sich. But if they'd jist let her alone, them Goodrich plant fellers and all, it would blow over. What few niggers come would not have stayed no duration. Not when they found she couldn't git the social stuff, and all."

And what the school superintendent, in middle Tennessee, had said: "You take a good many people around here that I know, segregationists all right, but when they read about a thousand to one, it sort of makes them sick. It is the unfairness in that way that gets them."

And an organizer of one of the important segregation groups, a lawyer, when I asked him if Autherine Lucy wasn't acting under law, he creaked his swivel chair, moved his shoulders under his coat, and touched a pencil on his desk, before saying: "Yes—yes—but it was just the Federal Court ruled it."

And a taxi driver in Nashville, a back-country man come to the city, a hard, lean, spare face, his lean, strong shoulders humped forward over the wheel so that the clavicles show through the coat: "A black-type person and a white-type person, they ain't alike. Now the black-type person, all they think about is fighting and having a good time and you know what. Now the white-type person is more American-type, he don't mind fighting but he don't fight to kill for fun. It's that cannibal blood you caint git out."

Now, on the plane, my companion observes me scribbling something in a notebook.

"You a writer or something?" he asks. "A news-paper fellow, maybe?"

I say yes.

"You interested in that stuff?" he asks, and

points to the article. "Somebody ought to tell 'em not to blame no state, not even Alabam' or Mississippi, for what the bad folks do. Like stuff in New York or Chicago. Folks in Mississippi got good hearts as any place. They always been nice and good-hearted to me, for I go up to a man affable. The folks down here is just in trouble and can't claw out. Don't blame 'em, got good hearts but can't claw out of their trouble. It is hard to claw out from under the past and the past way."

He asks me if I have been talking to a lot of people.

I had been talking to a lot of people.

◀

I had come to the shack at dusk, by the brim-
ming bayou, in the sea of mud where cotton had
been. The cold drizzle was still falling. In the
shack, on the hickory chair, the yellow girl, thin
but well made, wearing a salmon sweater and
salmon denim slacks, holds the baby on her knee
and leans toward the iron stove. On the table
beyond her is an ivory-colored portable radio
and a half-full bottle of Castoria. On the other
side of the stove are her three other children,
the oldest seven. Behind me, in the shadowy
background, I know there are faces peering in
from the other room of the shack, black faces,

13

the half-grown boys, another girl I had seen on entering. The girl in the salmon sweater is telling how she heard her husband had been killed. "Livin in town then, and my sister, she come that night and tole me he was shot. They had done shot him dead. So I up and taken out fer heah, back to the plantation. Later, my sister got my chillen and brought 'em. I ain't gonna lie, mister. I tell you, I was scairt. No tellin if that man what done it was in jail or no. Even if they had arrest him, they might bon' him out and he come and do it to me. Be mad because they 'rest him. You caint never tell. And they try him and 'quit him, doan know as I kin stay heah. Even they convick him, maybe I leave. Some good folks round heah and they helpin me, and I try to appreciate and be a prayin chile, but you git so bore down on and nigh ruint and sort of brain-washed, you don't know what. Things git to goin round in yore head. I could run out or somethin, but you caint leave yore chillen. But look like I might up and leave.

He git 'quitted, that man, and maybe I die, but I die goin."

This is the cliché. It is the thing the uninitiate would expect. It is the cliché of fear. It is the cliché come fresh, and alive.

There is another image. It is morning in Nashville. I walk down Union Street, past the Negro barber shops, past the ruinous buildings plastered over with placards of old circuses and rodeos, buildings being wrecked now to make way for progress, going into the square where the big white stone boxlike, ugly and expensive Davidson County Court House now stands on the spot where the old brawling market once was. Otherwise, the square hasn't changed much, the same buildings, wholesale houses, liquor stores, pawn shops, quick lunches, and the same kind of people stand on the corners, countrymen, in khaki pants and mackinaw coats, weathered faces and hard, withdrawn eyes, usually pale eyes, lean-hipped men ("narrow-assted" in the country phrase) like the men

15

who rode with Forrest, the farm wives, young
with a baby in arms, or middle-aged and work-
worn, with colored cloths over the head, glasses,
false teeth, always the shopping bag.

I walk down toward the river, past the Dar-
ling Display Distribution show window, where
a wax figure stands in skirt and silk blouse, the
fingers spread on one uplifted hand, the thin
face lifted with lips slightly parted as though in
eternal, tubercular expectation of a kiss. I see
the power pylons rising above the river mist. A
tug is hooting up-river in the mist.

I go on down to the right, First Street, to
the replica of Fort Nashborough, the original
settlement, which stands on the river bank under
the shadow of warehouses. The stockade looks
so child-flimsy and jerry-built jammed against
the massive, soot-stained warehouses. How
could the settlers have ever taken such protec-
tion seriously? But it was enough, that and their
will and the long rifles and the hunting knives
and the bear-dogs they unleashed to help them

16

when they broke the Indians at the Battle of the Bluffs. They took the land, and remain.

I am standing in the middle of the empty stockade when a boy enters and approaches me. He is about fifteen, strongly built, wearing a scruffed and tattered brown leather jacket, blue jeans, a faded blue stocking cap on the back of his head, with a mop of yellow hair hanging over his forehead. He is a fine-looking boy, erect, manly in the face, with a direct, blue-eyed glance. "Mister," he said to me, "is this foh't the way it was, or they done remodeled it?"

I tell him it is a replica, smaller than the original and not on the right spot, exactly.

"I'm glad I seen it, anyway," he says. "I like to go round seeing things that got history, and such. It gives you something to think about. Helps you in a quiz sometimes, too."

I ask him where he goes to school.

"Atlanta," he says. "Just come hitch-hiking up this a-way, looking at things for interest. Like this here foh't."

"You all been having a little trouble down your way," I ask, "haven't you?"

He looks sharply at me, hesitates, then says: "Niggers—you mean niggers?"

"Yes."

"I hate them bastards," he says, with a shuddering, automatic violence, and averts his face and spits through his teeth, a quick, viperish, cut-off expectoration.

I say nothing, and he looks at me, stares into my face with a dawning belligerence, sullen and challenging, and suddenly demands: "Don't you?"

"I can't say that I do," I reply. "I like some and I don't like some others."

He utters the sudden obscenity, and removes himself a couple of paces from me. He stops and looks back over his shoulder. "I'm hitching on back to Atlanta," he declares in a flat voice, "this afternoon," and goes on out of the fort.

This, too, is a cliché. The boy, standing on the ground of history and heroism, his intellect and imagination stirred by the fact, shudders with

that other, automatic emotion which my question had evoked. The cliché had come true: the
cliché of hate. And somehow the hallowedness
of the ground he stood on had vindicated, as
it were, that hate.

◄

The boy in the fort was the only person to turn
from me, but occasionally there would be a
stiffening, a flicker of suspicion, an evasion or
momentary refusal of the subject, even in the
casual acquaintance of lobby or barroom. At
one of the new luxurious motels near Clarksdale (the slick motels and the great power stations and booster stations, silver-glittering by

day and jewel-glittering by night, are the most obvious marks of the new boom), a well-dressed young man is talking about a movie being made down near Greenville. The movie is something about cotton, he says, by a fellow named Williams. Anyway, they had burned down a gin in the middle of the night, just for the movie. The woman at the desk (a very good blue dress that had cost money, a precise, respectable middle-aged mouth, pince-nez) speaks up: "Yes, and they say it's the only movie ever made here didn't criticize Mississippi."

"Criticize?" I ask. "Criticize how?"

She turns her head a little, looks at the man behind the desk with her, then back at me. "You know," she says, "just criticize."

I see the eyes of the man behind the desk stray to the license of our car parked just beyond the glass front. It has a Tennessee license, a U-Drive-It from Memphis.

"Criticize?" I try again.

The man had been busy arranging something in the drawer behind the desk. Suddenly, very

20

sharply, not quite slamming, he shoves the drawer shut. "Heck, you know," he says.

"Didn't they make another movie over at Oxford?" I ask.

The man nods, the woman says yes. I ask what that one had been about. Nobody had seen it, not the woman, neither of the men. "It was by that fellow Faulkner," the woman says. "But I never read anything he ever wrote."

"I never did either," the man behind the desk says, "but I know what it's like. It's like that fellow Hemingway. I read some of his writings. Gory and on the seedy side of life. I didn't like it."

"That's exactly right," the woman says, and nods. "On the seedy side of life. That fellow Faulkner, he's lost a lot of friends in Mississippi. Looking at the seedy side."

"Does he criticize?" I ask.

She turns away. The man goes through a door behind the desk. The well-dressed young man has long since become engrossed in a magazine.

◄

My Tennessee license, and Tennessee accent, hadn't been good enough credentials in Clarksdale, Mississippi. But on one occasion, the accent wasn't good enough even in Tennessee, and I remember sitting one evening in the tight, tiny living room (linoleum floor, gas heater, couch, one chair, small table with TV) of an organizer of a new important segregation group (one-time official of the Klan, this by court record) while he harangues me. He is a fat but powerful man, face fat but not flabby, the gray eyes squinty, set deep in the flesh, hard and sly by turns, never genial though the grin tries to be when

22

he has scored a point and leans forward at me, creaking the big overstuffed chair, his big hands crossed on his belly. He is a hill-man, come to town from one of the counties where there aren't too many Negroes, but he's now out to preserve, he says, "what you might name the old Southern way, what we was raised up to."

He is not out for money. ("I just git one dollar ever fellow I sign, the other two goes to Mr. Perkins at headquarters, for expense. Hell, I lose money on hit, on my gasoline.") No, he's not out for money, but something else. He is clearly a man of force, force that somehow has never found its way, and a man of language and leadership among his kind, the angry and ambitious and disoriented and dispossessed. It is language that intoxicates him now. He had been cautious at first, had thought I was from the FBI (yes, he had had a brush with them once, a perjury indictment), but now it seems some grand vista is opening before him and his eyes gleam and the words come.

He is talking too much, tangling himself. All

the while his wife (very handsome, almost beautiful, in fact, bobbed, disordered black hair
around a compact, smooth-chiseled, tanned face,
her body under a flimsy dress tight and compact but gracefully made) has been standing
in the deep shadow of the doorway to a room
beyond, standing patiently, hands folded but
tense, with the fingers secretly moving, standing like the proper hill-wife while the men-
folks talk.

"Excuse me," she suddenly says, but address-
ing me, not the husband, "excuse me, but didn't
you say you were born down here, used to live
right near here?"

I say yes.

She takes a step forward, coming out of the
shadow. "Yes," she says, "yes," leaning at me in
vindictive triumph, "but you never said where
you're living now!"

And I remember sitting with a group of college students, and one of them, a law student it
develops, short but strong-looking, dark-haired
and slick-headed, dark bulging eyes in a slick,

24

rather handsome, arrogant—no, bumptious—face, breaks in: "I just want to ask one question before anything starts. I just want to ask where you're from."

Suspicion of the outlander, or of the corrupted native, gets tangled up sometimes with suspicion of the New York press, but this latter suspicion may exist quite separately, on an informed and reasoned basis. For instance, I have seen a Southern newspaper man of high integrity and ability (an integrationist, by the way) suddenly strike down his fist and exclaim: "Well, by God, it's just a fact, it's not in them not to load the dice in a news story!" And another, a man publicly committed to maintaining law and order, publicly on record against the Citizens Councils and all such organizations: "*Life* magazine's editorial on the Till case, that sure fixed it. If Till's father had died a hero's death fighting for liberty, as *Life* said, that would have been as irrelevant as the actual fact that he was executed by the American army for rape-murder. It sure makes it hard."

There is the Baptist minister, an educated and intelligent man, who, when I show him an article in the *Reader's Digest*, an article mentioning that the Southern Baptist Convention had voted overwhelmingly for support of the Supreme Court decision, stiffens and says to me: "Look— look at that title!"

I didn't need to look. I knew what it was: "The Churches Repent."

But there is another suspicion story. A Negro told me this. A man from New Haven called on him, and upon being asked politely to take a chair, said, "Now, please, won't you tell me about the race problem."

To which the Negro replied: "Mister, I can't tell you a thing about that. There's nothing I could tell to you. If you want to find out, you better just move down here and live for a while."

That is the something else—the instinctive fear, on the part of black or white, that the massiveness of experience, the concreteness of life, will be violated; the fear of abstraction. I suppose it is this fear that made one man, a subtle and learned man, say to me: "There's something you can't explain, what being a Southerner is." And when he said that, I remembered a Yankee friend saying to me: "Southerners and Jews, you're exactly alike, you're so damned special."

"Yes," I said, "we're both persecuted minorities."

I had said it for a joke.

But had I?

◄

In the end people talked, even showed an anxiety to talk, to explain something. Even the black Southerners, a persecuted minority, too, would talk, for over and over the moment of some sudden decision would come: "All right— all right—I'll tell it to you straight. All right, there's no use beating around the bush."

But how fully can I read the words offered in the fullest effort of candor?

It is a town in Louisiana, and I am riding in an automobile driven by a Negro, a teacher, a slow, careful man, who puts his words out in that fashion, almost musingly, and drives his car that way, too. He has been showing me the Negro business section, how prosperous some of it is, and earlier he had said he would show me a section where the white men's cars almost line up at night. Now he seems to have forgotten that sardonic notion in the pleasanter, more prideful task. He has fallen silent, seemingly occupied with his important business of driving, and the car moves deliberately down the street. Then, putting his words out that slow way, detachedly as though I weren't there, he says: "You hear some white men say they know Negroes. Understand Negroes. But it's not true.

No white man ever born ever understood what a Negro is thinking. What he's feeling."

The car moves on down the empty street, negotiates a left turn with majestic deliberation.

"And half the time that Negro," he continues, "he don't understand, either."

I know that the man beside me had once, long back, had a bright-skinned, pretty wife. She had left him to be set up by a well-off white man (placée is the old word for it). The Negro man beside me does not know that I know this, but I have known it a long time, and now I wonder what this man is thinking as we ride along, silent again.

◀

Just listening to talk as it comes is best, but
sometimes it doesn't come, or the man says,
"You ask me some questions," and so, bit by bit,
a certain pattern of questions emerges, the old
obvious questions, I suppose—the questions
people respond to or flinch from.

*What are the white man's reasons for segrega-
tion?*

The man I am talking to is a yellow man,
about forty years old, shortish, rather fat, with
a very smooth, faintly Mongolian face, eyes very
shrewd but ready to smile. When the smile
really comes, there is a gold tooth showing, to

become, in that gold face, part of the sincerity of the smile. His arms seem somewhat short, and as he sits very erect in a straight chair, he folds his hands over his stomach. He gives the impression of a man very much at home in himself, at peace in himself, in his dignity, in his own pleasant, smooth-skinned plumpness, in some sustaining humorousness of things. He owns a small business, a shoe shop with a few employees.

"What does the white man do it for?" he rephrases the question. He pauses, and you can see he is thinking, studying on it, his smooth, yellow face compressing a little. All at once the face relaxes, a sort of humorous ripple, humorous but serious too, in a sort of wry way, before the face settles to its blandness. "You know," he says, "you know, years and years I look at some white feller, and I caint never figure him out. You go long with him, years and years, and all of a sudden he does something. I caint figure out what makes him do the way he does. It is like a mystery, you might say. I have studied on it."

31

Another Negro, a very black man, small-built
and intense, leans forward in his chair. He says
it is money, so the white man can have cheap
labor, can make the money. He is a bookish
man, has been to a Negro college, and though
he has never been out of the South, his speech
surprises me the way my native ear used to be
surprised by the speech of a Negro born and
raised, say, in Akron, Ohio. I make some fleet-
ing, tentative association of his speech, his education, his economic interpretation of things;
then let the notion slide.

"Yeah, yeah," the yellow man is saying, agree-
ing, "but—" He stops, shakes his head.

"But what?" I ask.

He hesitates, and I see the thumbs of the
hands lightly clasped across his belly begin to
move, ever so slowly, round and round each
other. "All right," he says, "I might as well say
it to you."

"Say what?"

"Mongrelization," he says, "that's what a
white man will say. You ask him and he'll say

32

that. He wants to head it off, he says. But—" He grins, the skin crinkles around his eyes, the grin shows the gold tooth. "But," he says, "look at my face. It wasn't any black man hung it on me."

The other man doesn't seem to think this is funny. "Yes," he says, "yes, they claim they don't want mongrelization. But who has done it? They claim Negroes are dirty, diseased, that that's why they want segregation. But they have Negro nurses for their children, they have Negro cooks. They claim Negroes are ignorant. But they won't associate with the smartest and best educated Negro. They claim—" And his voice goes on, winding up the bitter catalogue of paradoxes. I know them all. They are not new.

The smooth-faced, yellow man is listening. But he is thinking, too, the yellow blandness of his face creaming ever so little with his slow, humorous intentness. I ask him what he is thinking.

He grins, with philosophic ruefulness. "I was just studying on it," he says. "It's all true, what Mr. Elmo here says. But there must be something behind it all. Something he don't ever say, that white feller. Maybe—" He pauses, hunting for the formulation. "Maybe it's just prideful-ness," he says, "him being white."

Later, I am talking with the hill-man organizer, the one with the handsome wife who asks me where I live now, and he is telling me why he wants segregation. "The Court," he says, "hit caint take no stick and mix folks up like you swivel and swull eggs broke in a bowl. Naw," he says, "you got to raise 'em up, the niggers, not bring the white folks down to nigger level." He illustrates with his pudgy, strong hands in the air before him, one up, one down, changing levels. He watches the hands, with fascination, as though he has just learned to do a compli-cated trick.

How would you raise the level? I ask.

"Give 'em good schools, and things, yeah. But" —and he warms to the topic, leaning at me— "I'd 'bolish common law marriage. I'd put 'em in jail fer hit, and make 'em learn morals. Now a nigger don't know how to treat no wife, not even

34

a nigger wife. He whup her and beat her and maybe carve on her jaw with a pocketknife. When he ought to trick and pet her, and set her on his knee like a white man does his wife."

Then I talk with a Negro grade-school teacher, in the country, in Tennessee. She is a mulatto woman, middle-aged, with a handsome aquiline face, rather Indian-looking. She is sitting in her tiny, pridefully clean house, with a prideful bookcase of books beyond her, talking with slow and detached tones. I know what her story has been, years of domestic service, a painfully acquired education, marriage to a professional man, no children ("It was a cross to bear, but maybe that's why I love 'em so and like to teach 'em not my own").

I ask her why white people want to keep segregation.

"You ought to see the school house I teach in," she says, and pauses, and her lips curl sardonically, "set in the mud and hogs can come under it, and the privies set back in the mud. And see some of the children that come there, out of

35

homes with nothing, worse than the school house, no sanitation or cleanness, with disease and dirt and no manners. You wouldn't blame a white person for not wanting the white child set down beside them." Then with a slow movement of the shoulders, again the curl of the lips: "Why didn't the Federal Government give us money ten years ago for our school? To get ready, to raise us up a little to integrate. It would have made it easier. But now—"

But now? I ask.

"You got to try to be fair," she says.

I am talking with an official of one of the segregation outfits, late at night, in his house, in a fringe subdivision, in a small living room with red velvet drapes at the one window, a TV set, new, on a table, a plastic or plaster bas-relief of a fox hunter hung on the wall, in color, the hunting coat very red and arrogant. My host is seventy-five years old, bald except for a fringe of gray hair, sallow-skinned, very clean and scrubbed-looking, white shirt but no tie, a knife-edge crease to his hard-finish gray trousers. He smokes cigarettes, one after another, with nervous, stained fingers.

He was born in north Kentucky, romantically remembers the tobacco night riders ("Yeah, it was tight, nobody talked tobacco much, you might get shot"), remembers the Civil War veterans ("even the GAR's") sitting round, talking to the kids ("Yeah, they talked their war, they had something to remember and be proud of, not like these veterans we got nowadays, nothing to be proud of"), started out to be a lawyer ("But Blackstone got too dry, but history now, that's different, you always get something out of it to think about"), but wound up doing lots of things, finally, for years, a fraternal organizer.

Yes, he is definitely a pro, and when he talks of Gerald L. K. Smith he bursts out, eyes a-gleam: "Lord, that man's mailing list would be worth a million dollars!" He is not the rabble-rouser, the crusader, but the persuader, the debater, the man who gives the reasons. He is, in fact, a very American type, the old-fashioned, self-made, back-country intellectual—the type that finds apotheosis in Mark Twain and Abraham Lincoln. If he is neither of them, if he says "gondorea" and "enviro-mental" and "ethnolology," if something went wrong, if nothing ever came out quite right for him along the long way, you can still sense the old, unappeased hungers, the old drives of a nameless ambition. And he is sadly contemptuous of his organizers, who "aren't up to it," who "just aren't posted on history and ethnolology," who just haven't got "the old gray matter."

I ask him why the white man wants segregation.

"He'll say one thing and another," he says, "he knows in his bones it ain't right to have mixing. But you got to give him the reasons, explain it to him. It is the ethnolology of it you got to give. You got to explain how no *Negroes*"—he pronounces it with the elaborate polemical correctness, but not for polemics, just to set himself off intellectually, I suppose, from the people who might say *nigger*—"explain how no Negroes ever created a civilization. They are parasites. They haven't got the stuff up here." And he taps his forehead. "And explain how there is just two races, white and black, and—"

"What about the Bible," I ask, "doesn't the Bible say three?"

"Yes, but you know, between you and me, I don't reckon you have to take much stock in the Bible in this business. I don't take much stock in Darwin in some ways, either. He is too enviro-mental, he don't think enough about the blood. Yes, sir, I'll tell you, it's hard to come by good books on ethnolology these days. Got a good one from California the other day, though. But just one copy. Been out of print a long time. But like I was saying, the point is there's just two races, black and white, and the rest of them is a kind of mixing. You always get a mess when the mixing starts. Take India. They are a pure white people like you and me, and they had a pretty good civilization, too. Till they got to shipping on a little Negro blood. It don't take much to do the damage. Look at 'em now."

That is his argument. It is much the same argument given me by another official of another segregation group, whom I sit with a week later in another state, a lawyer, forty-five or -six, of strong middle height, sandy blond, hands strong with pale hairs and square-cut, scrubbed-looking nails. He is cagey at first, then suddenly warm, in an expanding, sincere, appealing way. He really wants to explain himself, wants to be regarded as an honest man, wants to be liked. I do like him, as he tells about himself, how he had gone to college, the hard way I gather, had prepared to be a teacher of history in high school, had given that up, had tried business in one way or another, had given that up, had studied law. "You ought to know my politics, too," he says. He was New Deal till the Court-packing plan. "That disgusted me," he says, and you believe him. Then he was for Willkie, then for Dewey, then Dixiecrat, then for Eisenhower. (I remember another lawyer, hired by another group: "Hell, all Southerners are Republicans at heart, conservative, and just don't know they're Republican.")

But Eisenhower doesn't satisfy my friend now. "We'll elect our own President. Our organization isn't just Southern. We're going national. Plenty of people in Chicago and other places feel like we do. And afraid of a big central government, too. We'll elect our own President and see how Chief Justice Warren's decision comes out."

I ask if the main point is the matter of States Rights, of local integrity.

"Yes, in a way," he says, "but you got to fight on something you can rouse people up about, on segregation. There's the constitutional argument, but your basic feeling, that's what you've got to trust—what you feel, not your reasons for it. But we've got argument, reasons."

He hesitates, thumps the desk top in a quick tattoo of his strong, scrubbed-looking fingers (he isn't a nervous man in the ordinary sense, but there are these sudden bursts), twists himself in his chair, then abruptly leans forward, jerks a drawer open (literally jerks it), and thrusts an envelope at me. "Heck, you might as well see it," he says.

I look at it. The stuff is not new. I have seen it before, elsewhere. It was used in the last gubernatorial campaign in Tennessee, it was used in the march on the Capitol at Nashville a few weeks ago. There are the handbills showing "Harlem Negro and White Wife," lying abed, showing "Crooner Roy Hamilton & Teenage Fans," who are white girls, showing a school yard in Baltimore with Negro and white children, "the new look in education." On the back of one of the handbills is a crudely drawn valentine-like heart, in it the head of a white woman who (with feelings not indicated by the artist) is about to be kissed by a black man of the most primitive physiognomy. On the heart two vultures perch. Beneath it is the caption: "The Kiss of Death."

Below are the "reasons": "While Russia makes laws to protect her own race she continues to

42

prod us to accept 14,000,000 Negroes as social equals and we are doing everything possible to please her. . . . Segregation is the law of God, not man. . . . Continue to rob the white race in order to bribe the Asiatic and Negro and these people will overwhelm the white race and destroy all progress, religion, invention, art, and return us to the jungle. . . . Negro blood destroyed the civilization of Egypt, India, Phoenecia, Carthage, Greece, and it will destroy America!"

I put the literature into my pocket, to join the other samples. "If there's trouble," I ask, "where will it begin?"

"We don't condone violence," he says.

"But if—just suppose," I say.

He doesn't hesitate. "The red-neck," he says, "that's what you call 'em around here. Those fellows—and I'm one of them myself, just a red-neck that got educated—are the ones who will feel the rub. He is the one on the underside of the plank with nothing between him and the

bare black ground. He's got to have something
to give him pride. Just to be better than something."

To be better than something: so we are back
to the pridefulness the yellow man had talked
about. But no, there is more, something else.

There is the minister, a Baptist, an intellec-
tual-looking man, a man whose face indicates
conscience and thoughtfulness, pastor of a good
· church in a good district in a thriving city. "It
is simple," he says. "It is a matter of God's will
and revelation. I refer you to Acts 17—I don't
remember the verse. This is the passage the
integrationists are always quoting to prove that
integration is Christian. But they won't quote it
all. It's the end that counts."

I looked it up: *And hath made of one blood
all nations of men for to dwell on all the face of
the earth, and hath determined the times before
appointed, and the bounds of their habitation.*

There is the very handsome lady of forty-five,
charming and witty and gay, full of dramatic
mimicry, a wonderful range of phrase, a quick

sympathy, a totally captivating talker of the kind you still occasionally find among women of the Deep South, but never now in a woman under forty. She is sitting before the fire in the fine room, her brother, big and handsome but barefoot and rigid drunk, opposite her. But she gaily overrides that small difficulty ("Oh, don't mind him, he's just had a whole bottle of brandy. Been on a high-lonesome all by himself. But poor Jack, he feels better now"). She has been talking about the Negroes on her plantation, and at last, about integration, but that only in one phrase, tossed off as gaily and casually as any other of the evening, so casual as to permit no discussion: "But of course we have to keep the white race intact."

But the husband, much her senior, who has said almost nothing all evening, lifts his strong, grizzled old face, and in a kind of *sotto voce* growl, not to her, not to me, not to anybody, utters: "In power—in power—you mean the white race in power."

And I think of another Southerner, an integrationist, saying to me: "You simply have to recognize a fact. In no county where the Negroes are two to one is the white man going to surrender political power, not with the Negroes in those counties in their present condition. It's not a question of being Southern. You put the same number of Yankee liberals in the same county and in a week they'd be behaving the same way. Living with something and talking about it are two very different things, and living with something is always the slow way."

And another, not an integrationist, from a black county, saying: "Yeah, let 'em take over and in six months you'd be paying the taxes but a black sheriff would be collecting 'em. You couldn't walk down the sidewalk. You'd be communized, all right."

But is it power? Merely power? Or any of the other things suggested thus far?

I think of a college professor in a section where about half the population is Negro. The college has no Negro students, but—"The heat is on," he says. "But listen, brother," he says, "lots of our boys don't like it a bit. Not a bit."

I ask would it be like the University of Alabama.

"It would be something, brother. I'll tell you that, brother. One of our boys—been fooling around with an organization uptown—he came to me and asked me to be sure to let him know when a nigger was coming, he and some friends would stop that clock. But I didn't want to hear student talk. I said, son, just don't tell me."

I asked what the faculty would do.

"Hide out, brother, hide out. And brother, I would, too."

Yes, he was a segregationist. I didn't have to ask him. Or ask his reasons, for he was talking on, in his rather nasal voice—leaning happily back in his chair in the handsome office, a spare, fiftyish man, dark-suited, rather dressy, sharp-nosed, with some fringe-remnants of sandy hair on an elongated, slightly freckled skull, rimless glasses on pale eyes: "Yeah, brother, back in my county there was a long ridge running through the county, and one side the ridge was good

47

land, river bottom, and folks put on airs there and held niggers, but on the other side of the ridge the ground so pore you couldn't grow peas and nothing but pore white trash. So when the Civil War came, the pore white trash, as the folks who put on airs called them, just picked down the old rifle off the deer horns over the fireplace and joined the Federals coming down, just because they hated those fellows across the ridge. But don't get me wrong, brother. They didn't want any truck with niggers, either. To this day they vote Republican and hate niggers. It is just they hate niggers."

Yes, they hate niggers, but I am in another room, the library of a plantation house, in Mississippi, and the planter is talking to me, leaning his length back at ease, speaking deliberately from his high-nosed, commanding face, the very figure of a Wade Hampton or Kirby Smith, only the gray uniform and cavalry boots not there, saying: "No, I don't hate Negroes. I never had a minute's trouble with one in my life, and never intend to. I don't believe in getting lathered up, and I don't intend to get lathered up. I simply don't discuss the question with anybody. But I'll tell you what I feel. I came out of the university with a lot of ideals and humanitarianism, and I stayed by it as long as I could. But I tell you now what has come out of thirty years of experience and careful consideration. I have a deep contempt for the Negro race as it exists here. It is not so much a matter of ability as of character. Character."

He repeats the word. He is a man of character, it could never be denied. Of character and force. He is also a man of fine intelligence and good education. He reads Roman history. He collects books on the American West. He is widely traveled. He is unusually successful as a planter and businessman. He is a man of human warmth and generosity, and eminent justice. I overhear his wife, at this moment, talking to a Negro from the place, asking him if she can save some more money for him, to add to the hundred dollars she holds, trying to persuade him.

The husband goes on: "It's not so much the

hands on my place, as the lawyers and doctors and teachers and insurance men and undertakers—oh, yes, I've had dealings all around, or my hands have. The character just breaks down. It is not dependable. They pay lip service to the white man's ideals of conduct. They say, yes, I believe in honesty and truth and morality. But it is just lip service. Most of the time. I don't intend to get lathered up. This is just my private opinion. I believe in segregation, but I can always protect myself and my family. I dine at my club and my land is my own, and when I travel, the places I frequent have few if any Negroes. Not that I'd ever walk out of a restaurant, for I'm no professional Southerner. And I'd never give a nickel to the Citizens Council or anything like that. Nor have any of my friends, that I know of. That's townpeople stuff, anyway."

Later on, he says: "For years, I thought I loved Negroes. And I loved their humor and other qualities. My father—he was a firster around here, first man to put glass windows in for them, first to give them a written monthly statement, first to do a lot to help them toward financial independence—well, my father, he used to look at me and say how it would be. He said, son, they will knock it out of you. Well, they did. I learned the grimness and the sadness."

And later, as we ride down the long row of the houses of the hands, he points to shreds of screening at windows, or here and there a broken screen door. "One of my last experiments," he says, dourly. "Three months, and they poked it out of the kitchen window so they could throw slops on the bare ground. They broke down the front door so they could spit tobacco juice out on the porch floor."

We ride on. We pass a nicely painted house, with a fenced dooryard, with flower beds, and flower boxes on the porch, and good, bright-painted porch furniture. I ask who lives there. "One of the hands," he says, "but he's got some energy and character. Look at his house. And he loves flowers. Has only three children, but when there's work he gets it done fast, and then finds some more to do. Makes $4,500 to $5,000 a year." Some old pride, or something from the lost days of idealism, comes back into his tone.

I ask what the other people on the place think of the tenant with the nice house.

"They think he's just lucky." And he mimics, a little bitterly, without any humor: "Boss, looks lak Jefferson's chillen, they jes picks faster'n mine. Caint he'p it, Boss."

I ask what Jefferson's color is.

"A real black man, a real Negro, all right. But he's got character."

I look down the interminable row of dingy houses, over the interminable flat of black earth toward the river.

◄

Now and then, I encounter a man whose argument for segregation, in the present context, has nothing to do with the Negro at all. At its simplest level its spokesman says: "I don't give a durn about the niggers, they never bother me one way or another. But I don't like being forced. Ain't no man ever forced me."

But the law always carries force, you say.

"Not this law. It's different. It ain't our law."

At another level, the spokesman will say it is a matter of constitutionality, pure and simple. He may even be an integrationist. But this decision, he will say, carries us one more step toward the power state, a cunningly calculated step, for this decision carries a moral issue and the objector to the decision is automatically put in the role of the enemy of righteousness. "But wait till the next decision," he will say. "This will be the precedent for it, and the next one won't have the moral façade."

Precedent for what? you ask.

"For government by sociology, not law," he will say.

"Is it government by law," one man asks me, "when certain members of the Supreme Court want to write a minority decision, and the great conciliator conciliates them out of it, saying that the thing is going to be controversial enough without the Court splitting? Damn it, the Court should split, if that's the honest reading of the law. We want the reading of the law, not conciliation by sociology. Even if we don't happen to like the kind of law it turns out to be in a particular case."

And another man: "Yes, government by sociology not law is a two-edged business. The next guy who gets in the saddle just picks another brand of sociology. And nothing to stop him, for the very notion of law is gone."

Pridefulness, money, level of intelligence, race, God's will, filth and disease, power, hate, contempt, legality—perhaps these are not all the words that get mentioned. There is another thing, whatever the word for it. An eminent Negro scholar is, I suppose, saying something about that other thing. "One thing," he says, "is that a lot of people down here just don't like change. It's not merely desegregation they're against so much, it's just the fact of any change. They feel some emotional tie to the way things are. A change is disorienting, especially if you're pretty disoriented already."

Yes, a lot of them are disoriented enough already, uprooted, driven from the land, drawn from the land, befuddled by new opportunities, new ambitions, new obligations. They have entered the great anonymity of the new world.

And I hear a college student in the Deep South: "You know, it's just that people don't like to feel like they're spitting on their grand-father's grave. They feel some connection they don't want to break. Something would bother them if they broke it."

The young man is, I gather, an integrationist. He adds: "And sometimes something bothers them if they don't break it."

Let us give a name now to whatever it is that the eminent Negro scholar and the young white college boy were talking about. Let us, without meaning to be ironical, call it piety.

◀

What does the Negro want?

The plump yellow man, with his hands folded calmly over his belly, the man who said it is the white man's "pridefulness," thinks, and answers the new question. "Opportunity," he says. "It's opportunity a man wants."

For what? I ask.

"Just to get along and make out. You know, like anybody."

"About education, now. If you got good schools, as good as anybody's, would that satisfy you?"

"Well," the yellow man begins, but the black, intense-faced man breaks in. "We never had them, we'd never have them!"

"You might get them now," I say, "under this pressure."

"Maybe," the yellow man agrees, "maybe. And it might have satisfied once. But"—and he shakes his head—"not now. That doctrine won't grip now."

"Not now," the intense-faced man says. "Not after the Supreme Court decision. We want the law."

"But when?" I ask. "Right now? Tomorrow morning?"

"The Supreme Court decision says—" And he stops.

"It says deliberate speed," I say, "or something like that."

"If a Negro wants to study medicine, he can't study it. If he wants to study law, he can't study it. There isn't any way in this state for him to study it."

"Suppose," I say, "suppose professional and graduate schools got opened. To really qualified applicants, no funny business either way. Then they began some sort of staggered system, a grade or two at a time, from either top or bottom. Would something like that satisfy you? Perhaps not all over the state at the same time, some place serving as a sort of pilot for others where the going would be rougher."

The yellow man nods. The intense-faced man looks down at his new and newly polished good black shoes. He looks across at the wall. Not looking at me, he says, "Yes, if it was in good faith. If you could depend on it. Yes."

58

He hates to say it. At least, I think he hates to say it. It is a wrench, grudging.

I sit in another room, in another city, in the Deep South, with several men, two of them Negroes. One Negro is the local NAACP secretary, a man in build, color and quality strangely like the black, intense-faced man. I am asking again what will satisfy the Negroes. Only this time the intense-faced man does not as readily say, yes, a staggered system would be satisfactory. In fact, he doesn't say it at all. I ask him what his philosophy of social change is, in a democracy. He begins to refer to the law, to the Court, but one of the white men breaks in.

This white man is of the Deep South, born, bred and educated there. He is a middle-aged man, tall, rather spare but not angular, the impression of the lack of angularity coming, I suppose, from a great deliberation in voice and movement, a great calmness in voice and face. The face is an intellectual's face, a calm, dedicated face, but not a zealot's. His career, I know, has been identified with various causes of social reform. He has sat on many committees, has signed many things, some of them things I personally take to be nonsense. What he says now, in his serene voice, the words and voice being really all that I know of him, is this: "I know that Mr. Cranford here"—and he nods toward this black, intense-faced man—"doesn't want any change by violence. He knows—we know—that change will take time. He wants a change in a Christian way that won't aggravate to violence. We have all got to live together. It will take time."

Nobody says anything. After a moment I go back to my question about the philosophy of social change. Wearily the intense-faced man says something, something not very relevant, not evasive, just not relevant. I let the matter drop. He sits with his head propped on his right hand, brow furrowed. He is not interested in abstractions. Why should he be?

Again, it is the Deep South, another town, another room, the bright, new-sparkling living room of the house of a Negro businessman, new furniture, new TV, new everything. There are several white men present, two journalists, myself (I've just come along to watch, I'm not involved), some technicians, and about ten Negroes, all in Sunday best, at ease but slightly formal, as though just before going in to a church service. Some of the Negroes, I have heard, are in the NAACP.

The technicians are rigging up their stuff, lights and cameras, etc., moving arrogantly in their own world, superior to human concerns. In the background, in the dining room, the wife of our host, a plump, fortyish mulatto, an agreeable-looking woman wearing a new black dress with a discreet white design in it, stands watching a big new electric percolator on a silver tray. Another silver tray holds a bottle of Canadian whisky, a good whisky, and glasses. When someone comes out of the kitchen, I catch a glimpse of a gray-haired Negro woman, wearing a maid's uniform.

It is a bright, sunny, crisp day outside. The

coffee is bubbling cheerfully. Out the window
I see a little Negro girl, about ten years old,
with a pink bow in her hair, an enormous bow,
come out of a small pink house with aquamarine
trim and shutters, and a dull blue roof. She
stands a moment with the pink bow against the
aquamarine door, then moves through the opening in the clipped privet hedge, a very tidy,
persnickety hedge, and picks her way down the
muddy street, where there is no sidewalk.

One of the journalists is instructing a Negro
who is to be interviewed, a tall, well-set-up, jut-
nosed, good-looking dark brown man in a blue
suit. He has a good way of holding his head.
"Now you're supposed to tell them," the journalist is saying, "what a lot of hogwash this separate but equal stuff is. What you said to me
last night."

Pedagogical and irritable, one of the technicians says: "Quiet, quiet!"

They take a voice level. The dark brown man
is very much at ease, saying: "Now is the time

for all good men to come to the aid of their country."

The interview begins. The dark brown man, still very much at ease, is saying: "—and we're not disturbed. The only people disturbed are those who have not taken an unbiased look. We who have taken our decision, we aren't disturbed." He goes on to say the Negroes want an interracial discussion on the "how" of desegregation—but with the background understanding that the Court decision is law.

The journalist cuts in: "Make it simple and direct. Lay it on the line."

The tall brown man is unruffled. There is sweat on his face now, but from the lamps. He wipes his face, and patiently, condescendingly, smiles at the journalist. "Listen," he says, "you all are going back to New York City. But we stay here. We aren't afraid, but we live here. They know what we think, but it's a way of putting it we got to think about."

He says it is going to take some time to work

63

things out, he knows that, but there is a chorus from the Negroes crowded back out of range of the camera: "Don't put no time limit—don't put any time on it—no ten or fifteen years!"

The dark brown man doesn't put any time on it. He says all they want is to recognize the law and to sit down in a law-abiding way to work out the "how" and the "when."

"That's good, that's all right!" the chorus decides.

Leave the "how" in detail up to the specialists in education. As for the "when"—the dark brown, jut-nosed man hesitates a second: "Well, Negroes are patient. We can wait a little while longer."

The dark brown man gets up to his considerable height, wipes the sweat off his face, asks the journalist: "You got your playback?"

The chorus laughs. It is indulgent laughter of human vanity and such. Sure, any man would like to hear his voice played back, hear himself talking.

There is no playback. Not now, anyway.

64

The dark brown man is receiving the hand-shakes, the shoulder-slaps, of his friends. They think he did well. He did do well. He looks back over his shoulder at the white men, grins. "When I got to leave," he says, "who's going to give me that job as chauffeur? I see that nice Cadillac sitting out front there."

There are the quick, deep-throated giggles.

I turn to a Negro beside me. "Ten years ago," I ask, "would this have been possible?"

"No," he says.

◄

Then there is another house, the tangle of wires, the jumble of rig and lights, and another Negro being arranged for an interview. There is no air of decorous festivity here, just a businesslike bustle, with the Negro waiting. This one will be knocked off quick. It's getting on to lunch.

This one, one of the journalists told me, is supposed to be the Uncle Tom. He is a middle-aged man, fair-sized, tallish, medium brown, with a balding, rather high forehead. He is wearing a good dark suit. His manner is dignified, slow, a little sad. I have known him before, know something about him. He had begun life as waterboy on a plantation, back in the times when "some folks didn't think a thing of bloodying a Negro's head, just for nothing, and I have seen their heads bloodied." But a white man on the plantation had helped him ("Noticed I was sort of quick and took an interest in things, trying to learn"), and now he is a preacher. For a voice level he does not say, "Now is the time for all good men to come to the aid of their country." He says: "Jesus wept, Jesus wept, Jesus wept."

The journalist tells him he is supposed to say some good things for segregation.

The Negro doesn't answer directly to that. "If you have some opinions of your own," he says, "your own people sometimes call you a son-of-a-gun, and sometimes the white people call you a son-of-a-gun."

Your own people. And I remember that the men at the last house had said: "Don't tell him you've seen us, don't tell him that or you won't get him to talk."

Is integration a good thing, the journalist asks him, and he says: "Till Negro people get as intelligent and self-sustaining they can't mix." But he flares up about discrimination along with segregation: "That's what makes Negroes bitter, wage differentials, no good jobs, that and the ballot." As for the Court decision, he says: "It's something for people to strive for, to ascertain their best."

I break in—I don't think the machinery is going yet—and ask about humiliation as a bar to Negro fulfilment.

"Segregation did one thing," he says. "No other race but the Negroes could build up as much will to go on and do things. To get their goals."

What goals? I ask.

"Just what anybody wants, just everything people can want to be a citizen," he says.

This isn't what the journalist has come for.

Things aren't promising too well. Uncle Tom is doing a disappearing act, Old Black Joe is evaporating, the handkerchief-head, most inconveniently, isn't there. The genie has got out of the bottle clearly labeled: *Negro* segregationist.

But maybe the genie can be coaxed back into the bottle. The sad-mannered man is, the journalist suggests, a pro-segregationist in that he thinks segregation built a will to achieve something.

The machinery gets going, the mike is lifted on its rod, the slow, sad voice speaks: "For segregation has test steel into the Negro race and this is one valuable point of segregation—segregation has proven that Negroes in the South, where it's practiced most, have done a fine job in building an economic strength beyond that of many other sections in the United States of America. Negroes own more farm land in Mississippi than any other state in the United States that is engaged in agriculture."

He goes along, he says, "with the idea you should have a moderate approach. You will never be able to integrate children on the school campus, the mothers holding a lot of bitterness in their hearts against each other white and colored."

It will take time, he says: "It is absurd otherwise, it's just foolish thinking for people to believe you can get the South to do in four or five years what they have been doing in the North for one hundred years. These people are emotional about their tradition, and you've got to have an educational program to change their way of thinking and this will be a slow process."

Yes, the genie is safely back in the labeled bottle. Or is he?

For the slow, sad voice is saying: "—has got to outthink the white man, has got to outlive the white man—"

Is saying: "—no need of saying the South won't ever integrate—"

Is saying: "—not ultimate goal just to go to white schools and travel with white people on conveyances over the country. No, the Negro, he is a growing people and he will strive for all the equailties belonging to any American citizen. He is a growing people."

Yes, Uncle Tom is gone again, and gone for good. Too bad for the program. I wondered if they got this last part on tape.

The Negro turns to the journalist and asks if he has interviewed other people around.

"Yes, saw Mr. So-and-so of the Citizens Council."

Had we interviewed any other Negroes?

"Oh, some," after a shade of hesitation.

Had we seen So-and-so and So-and-so?

"No—why, no. Well, we want to thank you—"

We leave the sad-mannered, slow man and we know that he knows. He isn't a big enough fool not to know. White men have lied to him before. What is one more time after all the years?

Besides, what if you do tell him a lie?

There are, as a matter of fact, in Arkansas, Negroes who go from door to door collecting money to fight integration. There *are* Uncle Toms.

So it all evens out.

◀

I ask my question of the eminent Negro scholar. His reply is immediate: "It's not so much what the Negro wants as what he doesn't want. The

71

main point is not that he has poor facilities. It is that he must endure a constant assault on his ego. He is denied human dignity."

And I think of the yellow girl wearing the salmon sweater and slacks, in the shack in the sea of mud, at dusk, the girl whose husband has been shot, and she says: "It's how yore feelings git tore up all the time. The way folks talk, sometimes. It ain't what they say sometimes, if they'd jes say it kind."

She had gone to a store, in another town, for some dress goods, and had requested a receipt for the minister who manages the fund raised in her behalf. By the receipt the saleswoman identifies her and asks if "that man up yonder is still in jail for killing a nigger."

"Well," the girl has said, "if you want to put it that a-way."

"They can't do anything to a man for something he does drunk," the saleswoman has said.

The girl has laid the package down on the counter. "If you want it that a-way," she has said, "you kin take back yore dress goods. They's other places to buy."

She tells me the story.

And I think of another woman, up in Tennessee, middle-aged, precise, the kind of woman who knows her own competent mind, a school inspector for county schools, a Negro. "We don't want to socialize. That's not what we want. We do everything the white folks do already, even if we don't spend as much money doing it. And we have more fun. But I don't want to be insulted. If somebody has to tell you something, about some regulation or other, they could say it in a low, kind voice, not yell it out at you. And when I go to a place to buy something, and have that dollar bill in my hand, I want to be treated right. And I won't ride on a bus. I won't go to a restaurant in a town where there's just one. I'll go hungry. I won't be insulted at the front door and then crawl around to the back. You've got to try to keep some respect."

And in Tennessee again, the Negro at the bi-racial committee meeting says: "My boy is happy in the Negro school where he goes. I don't want him to go to the white school and sit by your boy's side. But I'd die fighting for his right to go."

◀

"We don't want to socialize," the woman in Tennessee says.

The college student, a Negro, in Tennessee, says: "The Negro doesn't want social equality. My wife is my color. I'm above wanting to mix things up. That's low class. Low class of both races."

74

The Negro man in Mississippi says: "Take a
Negro man wanting a white woman. A man
tends to want his own kind, now. But the white
folks make such an awful fuss about it. They
make it seem so awful special-like. Maybe that's
what makes it sort of prey on some folks' mind."

And I remember the gang rape by four Negroes of a white woman near Memphis last fall,
shortly after the Till killing. "One of our boys
was killed down in Mississippi the other day
and we're liable to kill you," one of the Negroes
said as they bludgeoned the man who was with
the woman and told him to get going.

◀

This is a question for Negroes only. *Is there any difference between what the Negro feels at the exclusions of segregation, and what a white man feels at the exclusions which he, any man, must always face at some point?*

"Yes, it's different," the Negro college administrator says, "when your fate is on your face. Just that. It's the unchangeableness. Now a white man, even if he knows he can't be President, even if he knows the chances for his son are one in many millions—long odds—still there's an idea there."

And the Negro lawyer: "Yes, it's different. But

it's not easy to name it. Take how some unions come in and make some plant build nice rest rooms, one for white, one for Negroes, but same tile, same fixtures and all. But off the white ones, there's a little lounge for smoking. To make 'em feel superior to somebody. You see what I mean, how it's different?"

He thinks some more. "Yes," he says, "I got my dreams and hopes and aspirations, but me, I have to think what is sort of possible in the possibilities and probabilities. Some things I know I can't think on because of the circumstances of my birth."

And he thinks again, looking out the window, over Beale Street. "Yes, there's a difference," he says. "A Negro, he doesn't really know some things, but he just goes walking pregnant with worries, not knowing their name. It's he's lost his purpose, somewhere. He goes wandering and wondering, and no purpose."

I look out the window, too, over Beale Street. It is late afternoon. I hear the pullulation of life, the stir and new tempo toward evening, the babble of voices, a snatch of laughter. I hear the remorseless juke boxes. They shake the air.

◀

What's coming?

"Whatever it is," the college student in the Deep South says, "I'd like to put all the Citizens Council and all the NAACP in one room and give every man a baseball bat and lock 'em in till it was over. Then maybe some sensible people could work out something."

What's coming? I say it to the country grade-school superintendent. He is a part-time farmer, too, and now he is really in his role as farmer, not teacher, as we stand, at night, under the naked light of a flyspecked 200-watt bulb hanging from the shed roof, and he oversees two

Negroes loading sacks of fertilizer on a truck. "I know folks round here," he says, and seeing his hard, aquiline, weathered face, with the flat, pale, hard eyes, I believe him.

"They aren't raised up to it," he says. "Back in the summer now, I went by a lady's house to ask about her children starting to school. Well, she was a real old-timey gal, a gant-headed, barefoot, snuff-dipping, bonnet-wearing, hard-ankled old gal standing out in the tobacco patch, leaning on her hoe, and she leaned at me and said, 'Done hear'd tell 'bout niggers gonna come in,' and before I could say anything, she said, 'Not with none of my young 'uns,' and let out a stream of ambeer."

"Would you hire a Negro teacher?" I asked.

"I personally would, but folks wouldn't stand for it, not now, mostly those who never went much to school themselves. Unless I could prove I couldn't get white." He paused. "And it's getting damned hard to get white, I tell you," he says.

I ask if integration will come.

"Sure," he says, "in fifty years. Every time the tobacco crop is reduced, we lose just that many white sharecroppers and Negroes. That eases the pain."

What's coming? And the Methodist minister, riding with me in the dusk, in the drizzle, by the flooded bayou, says: "It'll come, desegregation and the vote and all that. But it will be twenty-five, thirty years, a generation. You can preach love and justice, but it's a slow pull till you get the education." He waves a hand toward the drowned black cotton fields, stretching on forever, toward the rows of shacks marshaled off into the darkening distance, toward the far cypresses where dusk is tangled. "You can see," he says. "Just look, you can see."

What's coming? I ask the young lawyer in a mid-South city, a lawyer retained by one of the segregation outfits. "It's coming that we got to fight this bogus law," he says, "or we'll have a lot of social dis-tensions. The bogus law is based on social stuff and progress and just creates dis-tension. But we're gaining ground. Some upper-class people, I mean a real rich man, is coming out for us. And we get rolling, a Southern President could repack the court. But it's got so a man can't respect the Supreme Court. All this share-the-wealth and Communist stuff and progress. You can't depend on law any more."

What can you depend on? I ask.

"Nothing but the people. Like the Civil War."

I suggest that whatever the constitutional rights and wrongs of the Civil War were, we had got a new Constitution out of it.

"No," he said, "just a different type of dog saying what it is."

I ask if, in the end, the appeal would be to violence.

"No, I don't believe in violence. I told Mr. Perkins, when we had our mass meeting, to keep the in-ci-dents down. But you get a lot of folks and there's always going to be in-ci-dents."

I ask if at Tuscaloosa the mob hadn't dictated public policy.

"Not dictate exactly." And he smiles his handsome smile. "But it was a lot of people."

He has used the word *progress,* over and over, to damn what he does not like. It is peculiar how he uses this laudatory word—I can imagine how he would say it in other contexts, on public occasions, rolling it on his tongue—as the word now for what he hates most. I wonder how deep a cleavage the use of that word indicates.

What's coming? I ask the handsome, aristocratic, big gray-haired man, sitting in his rich office, high over the city, an ornament of the vestry, of boards of directors, of club committees, a man of exquisite simplicity and charm, and a member of a segregation group.

"We shall exhaust all the legal possibilities," he says.

I ask if he thinks his side will win. The legal fight, that is.

He rolls a cigarette fastidiously between strong, white, waxy forefinger and thumb. "No," he says. "But it is just something you have to do." He rolls the cigarette, looking out the window over the city, a city getting rich now, "filthy rich," as somebody has said to me. There is the undertone and unceasing susurrus of traffic in the silence of his thoughts.

"Well," he says at last, "to speak truth, I think the whole jig is up. We'll have desegregation right down the line. And you know why?"

I shake my head.

"Well, I'll tell you. You see those girls in my office outside, those young men. Come from good lower-middle-class homes, went to college a lot of them. Well, a girl comes in here and says to me a gentleman is waiting. She shows him in. He is as black as the ace of spades. It just never crossed that girl's mind, what she was saying, when she said a gentleman was waiting." He pauses. "Yes, sir," he says, "I just don't know why I'm doing it."

I am thinking of walking down Canal Street, in New Orleans, and a man is saying to me: "Do you know how many millions a year the Negroes spend up and down this street?"

No, I had said, I didn't know.

He tells me the figure, then says: "You get the logic of that, don't you?"

What's coming? And the college student says:
"I'll tell you one thing that's coming, there's not
going to be any academic freedom or any other
kind around here if we don't watch out. Now
I'm a segregationist, that is, the way things are
here right now, but I don't want anybody saying
I can't listen to somebody talk about something.
I can make up my own mind."

What's coming? And a state official says: "Integration sure and slow. A creeping process. If
the NAACP has got bat sense, not deliberately
provoking things as in the University of Alabama deal. They could have got that girl in
quiet and easy, but that wouldn't satisfy them.
No, they wanted the bang. As for things in gen-
eral, grade schools and high schools, it'll be the
creeping process. The soft places first, and then
one county will play football or basketball with
Negroes on the team. You know how it'll be. A
creeping process. There'll be lots of court actions, but don't let court actions fool you. I bet
you half the superintendents over in Tennessee
will secretly welcome a court action in their

county. Half of 'em are worried morally and half financially, and a court action just gets 'em off the hook. They didn't initiate it, they can always claim, but it gets them off the hook. That's the way I would feel, I know."

What's coming? I ask the taxi driver in Memphis. And he says: "Lots of dead niggers round here, that's what's coming. Look at Detroit, lots of dead niggers been in the Detroit River, but it won't be a patch on the Ole Mississippi. But hell, it won't stop nothing. Fifty years from now everybody will be gray anyway, Jews and Germans and French and Chinese and niggers, and who'll give a durn?"

The cab has drawn to my destination. I step out into the rain and darkness. "Don't get yourself drownded now," he says. "You have a good time now. I hope you do."

What's coming? And a man in Arkansas says: "We'll ride it out. But it looked like bad trouble one time. Too many outsiders. Mississippians and all. They come back here again, somebody's butt will be busted."

85

And another man: "Sure, they aim for violence, coming in here. When a man gets up before a crowd and plays what purports to be a
recording of an NAACP official, an inflamma-
tory sex thing, and then boasts of having been
in on a lynching himself, what do you call it?
Well, they got him on the witness stand, under
oath, and he had to admit he got the record
from Patterson, of the Citizens Council, and admitted under oath the lynching statement. He
also admitted under oath some other interesting
facts—that he had once been indicted for crim-
inal libel but pleaded guilty to simple libel, that
he has done sixty days for contempt of court
on charges of violating an injunction having to
do with liquor. Yeah, he used to run a paper
called *The Rub Down*—that's what got him into
the libel business. What's going to happen if a
guy like that runs things? I ask you."

What's coming? And the planter leans back
with the glass in his hand. "I'm not going to get
lathered up," he says, "because it's no use. Why
is the country so lathered up to force the issue

one way or the other? Democracy—democracy
has just come to be a name for what you like. It
has lost responsibility, no local integrity left, it
has been bought off. We've got the power state
coming on, and communism or socialism, whatever you choose to call it. Race amalgamation is
inevitable. I can't say I like any of it. I am out
of step with the times."

What's coming? I ask the Episcopal rector, in
the Deep South, a large handsome man, almost
the twin of my friend sitting in the fine office
overlooking the rich city. He has just told me
that when he first came down from the North, a
generation back, his bishop had explained it all
to him, how the Negroes' skull capacity was lim-
ited. But as he has said, brain power isn't everything, there's justice, and not a member of his
congregation wasn't for conviction in the Till
case.

"But the Negro has to be improved before integration," he says. "Take their morals, we are
gradually improving the standard of morality
and decency."

The conversation veers, we take a longer view. "Well, anthropologically speaking," he says, "the solution will be absorption, the Negro will disappear."

I ask how this is happening.

"Low-class people, immoral people, libertines, wastrels, prostitutes and such," he says.

I ask if, in that case, the raising of the moral level of the Negro does not prevent, or delay, what he says is the solution.

The conversation goes into a blur.

What's coming? And the young man from Mississippi says: "Even without integration, even with separate but pretty good facilities for the Negro, the Negro would be improving himself. He would be making himself more intellectually and socially acceptable. Therefore, as segregationists, if we're logical, we ought to deny any good facilities to them. Now I'm a segregationist, but I can't be that logical."

What's coming? And the officer of the Citizens Council chapter says: "Desegregation, integration, amalgamation—none of it will come here. To say it will come is defeatism. It won't come if we stand firm."

And the old man in north Tennessee, a burly, full-blooded, red-faced, raucous old man, says: "Hell, son, it's easy to solve. Just blend 'em. Fifteen years and they'll all be blended in. And by God, I'm doing my part!"

◄

Out of Memphis, I lean back in my seat on the plane, and watch the darkness slide by. I know what the Southerner feels going out of the South, the relief, the expanding vistas. Now, to the sound of the powerful, magnanimous engines bearing me through the night, I think of that, thinking of the new libel laws in Mississippi, of the academic pressures, of academic resignations, of the Negro facing the shotgun blast, of the white man with a nice little, hard-built business being boycotted, of the college boy who said: "I'll just tell you, everybody is *scairt.*"

I feel the surge of relief. But I know what the relief really is. It is the relief from responsibility.

Now you may eat the bread of the Pharisee and read in the morning paper, with only a trace of irony, how out of an ultimate misery of rejection some Puerto Rican school boys—or is it Jews or Negroes or Italians?—who call themselves something grand, The Red Eagles or the Silver Avengers, have stabbed another boy to death, or raped a girl, or trampled an old man into a bloody mire. If you can afford it, you will, according to the local mores, send your child to a private school, where there will be, of course, a couple of Negro children on exhibit. And that delightful little Chinese girl who is so good at dramatics. Or is it finger painting?

Yes, you know what the relief is. It is the flight from the reality you were born to.

◀

But what is that reality you have fled from?

It is the fact of self-division. I do not mean division between man and man in society. That division is, of course, there, and it is important. Take, for example, the killing of Clinton Melton, in Glendora, Mississippi, in the Delta, by a man named Elmer Kimbell, a close friend of Milam (who had been acquitted of the murder of Till, whose car was being used by Kimbell at the time of the killing of Melton, and to whose house Kimbell returned after the deed).

Two days after the event, twenty-one men

—storekeepers, planters, railroad men, school teachers, preacher, bookkeepers—sent money to the widow for funeral expenses, with the note: "Knowing that he was outstanding in his race, we the people of this town are deeply hurt and donate as follows." When the Lions Club met three days after the event, a resolution was drawn and signed by all members present: "We consider the taking of the life of Clinton Melton an outrage against him, against all the people of Glendora, against the people of Mississippi as well as against the entire human family. . . . We humbly confess in repentance for having so lived as a community that such an evil occurrence could happen here, and we offer ourselves to be used in bringing to pass a better realization of the justice, righteousness and peace which is the will of God for human society."

And the town began to raise a fund to realize the ambition of the dead man, to send his children to college, the doctor of Glendora offered employment in his clinic to the widow, and the owner of the plantation where she had been raised offered to build for her and her children a three-room house.

But, in that division between man and man, the jury that tried Elmer Kimbell acquitted him.

But, in that same division between man and man, when the newspaper of Clarksdale, Mississippi, in the heart of the Delta, ran a front-page story of the acquittal, that story was bracketed with a front-page editorial saying that there had been some extenuation for acquittal in the Till case, with confusion of evidence and outside pressures, but that in the Melton case there had been no pressure and "we were alone with ourselves and we flunked it."

Such division between man and man is important. As one editor in Tennessee said to me: "There's a fifth column of decency here, and it will, in the end, betray the extremists, when the politicians get through." But such a division between man and man is not as important in the long run as the division within the individual man.

93

Within the individual there are, or may be, many lines of fracture. It may be between his own social idealism and his anger at Yankee Phariseeism. (Oh, yes, he remembers that in the days when Federal bayonets supported the black Reconstruction state governments in the South, not a single Negro held elective office in any Northern state.) It may be between his social views and his fear of the power state. It may be between his social views and his clan sense. It may be between his allegiance to organized labor and his racism—for status or blood purity. It may be between his Christianity and his social prejudice. It may be between his sense of democracy and his ingrained attitudes toward the Negro. It may be between his own local views and his concern for the figure America cuts in the international picture. It may be between his practical concern at the money loss to society caused by the Negro's depressed condition and his own personal gain or personal prejudice. It may be, and disastrously, between

94

his sense of the inevitable and his emotional need to act against the inevitable.

There are almost an infinite number of permutations and combinations, but they all amount to the same thing, a deep intellectual rub, a moral rub, anger at the irremediable self-division, a deep exacerbation at some failure to find identity. That is the reality.

It expresses itself in many ways. I sit for an afternoon with an old friend, a big, weather-faced, squarish man, a farmer, an intelligent man, a man of good education, of travel and experience, and I ask him questions. I ask if he thinks we can afford, in the present world picture, to alienate Asia by segregation here at home. He hates the question. "I hate to think about it," he says. "It's too deep for me," he says, and moves heavily in his chair. We talk about Christianity—he is a church-going man—and he says: "Oh, I know what the Bible says, and Christianity, but I just can't think about it. My mind just shuts up."

My old friend is an honest man. He will face his own discomfort. He will not try to ease it by passing libel laws to stop discussion or by firing professors.

There are other people whose eyes brighten at the thought of the new unity in the South, the new solidarity of resistance. These men are idealists, and they dream of preserving the traditional American values of individualism and localism against the anonymity, irresponsibility and materialism of the power state, against the philosophy of the ad-man, the morality of the Kinsey report, and the gospel of the bitch-goddess. *To be Southern again:* to recreate a habitation for the values they would preserve, to achieve in unity some clarity of spirit, to envisage some healed image of their own identity.

Some of these men are segregationists. Some are desegregationists, but these, in opposing what they take to be the power-state implications of the Court decision, find themselves caught, too, in the defense of segregation. And

defending segregation, both groups are caught
in a paradox: in seeking to preserve individualism by taking refuge in the vision of a South
redeemed in unity and antique virtue, they are
fleeing from the burden of their own individuality—the intellectual rub, the moral rub. To state
the matter in another way, by using the argument of *mere* social continuity and the justifica-
tion by mere *mores,* they think of a world in
which circumstances and values are frozen; but
the essence of individuality is the willingness to
accept the rub which the flux of things pro-
vokes, to accept one's fate in time. What heroes
would these idealists enshrine to take the place
of Jefferson and Lee, those heroes who took the
risk of their fate?

Even among these people some are in discomfort, discomfort because the new unity, the new
solidarity, once it descends from the bright
world of Idea, means unity with some quite concrete persons and specific actions. They say:
"Yes—yes, we've got to unify." And then: "But
we've got to purge certain elements."

But who will purge whom? And what part of yourself will purge another part?

"Yes, it's our own fault," the rich businessman, active in segregation, says. "If we'd ever managed to bring ourselves to do what we ought to have done for the Negro, it would be different now, if we'd managed to educate them, get them decent housing, decent jobs."

So I tell him what a Southern Negro professor had said to me. He had said that the future now would be different, would be hopeful, if there could just be "one gesture of graciousness" from the white man—even if the white man didn't like the Supreme Court decision, he might try to understand the Negro's view, not heap insult on him.

And the segregationist, who is a gracious man, seizes on the word. "Graciousness," he says, "that's it, if we could just have managed some graciousness to the race. Sure, some of us, a lot of us, could manage some graciousness to individual Negroes, some of us were grateful to individuals for being gracious to us. But you know, we couldn't manage it for the race." He thinks a moment, then says: "There's a Negro woman buried in the family burial place. We loved her."

I believe him when he says it. And he sinks into silence, feeling the rub, for the moment anyway, between the man who can talk in terms of graciousness, in whatever terms that notion may present itself to him, and the man who is a power for segregation.

This is the same man who has said to me, earlier, that he knows integration to be inevitable, doesn't know why he is fighting it. But such a man is happier, perhaps, than those men, destined by birth and personal qualities to action and leadership, who in the face of what they take to be inevitable feel cut off from all action. "I am out of step with the times," one such man says to me, and his wife says, "You know, if we feel the way we do, we ought to do something about it," and he, in some deep, inward, unproclaimed bitterness, says, "No, I'm not going to get lathered up about anything."

Yes, there are many kinds of rub, but I suppose that the commonest one is the moral one—the Christian one, in fact, for the South is still a land of faith. There is, of course, the old joke that after the Saturday night lynching, the congregation generally turns up a little late for church, and the sardonic remark a man made to me about the pro-integration resolution of the Southern Baptist Convention: "They were just a little bit exalted. When they got back with the home folks a lot of 'em wondered how they did it."

But meanwhile, there are the pastors at Glendora and Hoxie and Oxford and other nameless places. And I remember a pastor, in Tennessee, a Southerner born and bred, saying to me: "Yes, I think the Court decision may have set back race equality—it was coming fast, faster than anybody could guess, because so quiet. But now some people get so put out with the idea of Negroes in church, they stop me on the street and say if I ever let one in they won't come to church. So I ask about Heaven, what will they do in Heaven?

"'Well,' one woman said, 'I'll just let God segregate us.'

"'You'll *let* God segregate you?' I said, and she flounced off. But I ask, where is Christianity if people can't worship together? There's only one thing to try to preach, and that is Christ. And there's only one question to ask, and that is what would Christ do?"

Will they go with him, I ask.

"They are good Christian people, most of them," he says. "It may be slow, but they are Christians."

And in a town in south Kentucky, in a "black county," a Confederate county, where desegregation is now imminent in the high schools, the superintendent says to me: "The people here are good Christian people, trying to do right. When this thing first came up, the whole board said

they'd walk out. But the ministers got to preach-
ing, and the lawyers to talking on it, and they
came around."

I asked how many were influenced by moral,
how many by legal, considerations.

About half and half, he reckons, then adds:
"I'm a Rebel myself, and I don't deny it, but I'm
an American and a law-abiding citizen. A man
can hate an idea but know it's right, and it takes
a lot of thinking and praying to bring yourself
around. You just have to uncover the unrecog-
nized sympathy in the white man for the Negro
humiliation."

Fifty miles away I shall sit in a living room
and hear some tale of a Negro coming to somebody's front door—another house—and being
admitted by a Negro servant and being found
by the master of the house, who says: "I don't
care if Susie did let you in. I don't care if Jesus
Christ let you in. No black son-of-a-bitch is coming to my front door."

After the tale, there is silence. All present are
segregationist, or I think they are.

Then one woman says: "Maybe he did take a lot on himself, coming to the front door. But I can't stand it. He's human."

And another woman: "I think it's a moral question, and I suffer, but I can't feel the same way about a Negro as a white person. It's born in me. But I pray I'll change."

The successful businessman in Louisiana says to me: "I have felt the moral question. It will be more moral when we get rid of segregation. But I'm human enough—I guess it's human to be split up—to want things just postponed till my children are out of school. But I can't lift my finger to delay things."

But this man, privately admitting his division of feeling, having no intention of public action on either side, is the sort of man who can be trapped, accidentally, into action.

There is the man who got the letter in the morning mail, asking him to serve as chairman of a citizens committee to study plans for desegregation in his county. "I was sick," he says, "and I mean literally sick. I felt sick all day. I

103

didn't see how I could get into something like that. But next morning, you know, I did it."

That county now has its schedule for desegregation.

There is another man, a lawyer, who has been deeply involved in a desegregation action. "I never had much feeling of prejudice, but hell, I didn't have any theories either, and I now and then paid some lip service to segregation. I didn't want to get mixed up in the business. But one night a telephone call came. I told the man I'd let him know next day. You know, I was sick. I walked on back in the living room and my wife looked at me. She must have guessed what it was. 'You going to do it?' she asked me. I said, hell, I didn't know, and went out. I was plain sick. But next day I did it. Well," he says, and grins, and leans back under the shelves of law books, "and I'm stuck with it. But you know, I'm getting damned tired of the paranoiacs and illiterates I'm up against."

Another man, with a small business in a poor county, "back in the shelf country," he calls it, a short, strong-looking, ovoidal kind of man with his belt cutting into his belly when he leans back in his office chair. He is telling me what he has been through. "I wouldn't tell you a lie," he says. "I'm Southern through and through, and I guess I got every prejudice a man can have, and I certainly never would have got mixed up in this business if it hadn't been for the Court decision. I wouldn't be out in front. I was just trying to do my duty. Trying to save some money for the county. I never expected any trouble. And we might not have had any if it hadn't been for outsiders, one kind and another.

"But what nobody understands is how a man can get cut up inside. You try to live like a Christian with your fellow man, and suddenly you find out it is all mixed up. You put in twenty-five years trying to build up a nice little business and raise up a family and it looks like it will all be ruined. You get word somebody will dynamite your house and you in it. You go to lawyers and they say they sympathize, but nobody'll take your case. But the worst is, things just go round and round in your head. Then they won't come a-tall, and you lay there in the night. You might say, it's the psychology of it you can't stand. Getting all split up. Then, all of a sudden, somebody stops you on the street and calls you something, a so-and-so nigger-lover. And you know, I got so mad not a thing mattered any more. I just felt like I was all put back together again."

He said he wished he could write it down, how awful it is for a man to be split up.

◀

Negroes, they must be split up, too, I think. They are human, too. There must be many ways for them to be split up. I remember asking a

Negro school teacher if she thought Negro resentment would be a bar to integration. "Some of us try to teach love," she says, "as well as we can. But some of us teach hate. I guess we can't help it."

Love and hate, but more than that, the necessity of confronting your own motives: *Do we really want to try to work out a way to live with the white people or do we just want to show them, pay off something, show them up, rub their noses in it?*

And I can imagine the grinding anger, the sense of outrage of a Negro crying out within himself: *After all the patience, after all the humility, after learning and living those virtues, do I have to learn magnanimity, too?*

Yes, I can imagine the outrage, the outrage as some deep, inner self tells him, yes, he must.

I am glad that white people have no problem as hard as that.

◀

The taxi drew up in front of the apartment house, and I got out, but the driver and I talked on for a moment. I stood there in the rain, then paid him, and ran for the door. It wasn't that I wanted to get out of the rain. I had an umbrella. I wanted to get in and write down what he had said.

He was a local man, born near Nashville, up near Goodlettsville, "raised up with niggers." He had been in the army, with lots of fighting, Africa, Sicily, Italy, but a lot of time bossing work gangs. In Africa, at first, it had been Arabs, but Arabs weren't "worth a durn." Then they got Negro work battalions.

108

But here are the notes:

Niggers a lot better than Arabs, but they didn't hurt themselves—didn't any of 'em git a hernia for Uncle Sam—race prejudice—but it ain't our hate, it's the hate hung on us by the old folks dead and gone. Not I mean to criticize the old folks, they done the best they knew, but that hate, we don't know how to shuck it. We got that God-damn hate stuck in our craw and can't puke it up. If white folks quit shoving the nigger down and calling him a nigger he could maybe get to be a asset to the South and the country. But how stop shoving?

We are the prisoners of our history.

Or are we?

◄

There is one more interview I wish to put on record. I shall enter it by question and answer.

Q. You're a Southerner, aren't you?

A. Yes.

Q. Are you afraid of the power state?

A. Yes.

Q. Do you think the Northern press sometimes distorts Southern news?

A. Yes.

Q. Assuming that they do, why do they do it?

A. They like to feel good.

Q. What do you think the South ought to do about that distortion?

110

A. Nothing.

Q. Nothing? What do you mean, nothing?

A. The distortion—that's the Yankees' problem, not ours.

Q. You mean they ought to let the South work out a way to live with the Negro?

A. I don't think the problem is to learn to live with the Negro.

Q. What is it then?

A. It is to learn to live with ourselves.

Q. What do you mean?

A. I don't think you can live with yourself when you are humiliating the man next to you.

Q. Don't you think the races have made out pretty well, considering?

A. Yes. By some sort of human decency and charity, God knows how. But there was always an image of something else.

Q. An image?

A. Well, I knew an old lady who grew up in a black county, but a county where relations had been, as they say, good. She had a fine farm and a good brick house, and when she got old she

sort of retired from the world. The hottest summer weather and she would lock all the doors
and windows at night, and lie there in the airless
dark. But sometimes she'd telephone to town in
the middle of the night. She would telephone
that somebody was burning the Negroes out
there on her place. She could hear their screams.
Something was going on in her old head which
in another place and time would not have been
going on in her old head. She had never, I
should think, seen an act of violence in her life.
But something was going on in her head.

Q. Do you think it is chiefly the red-neck who
causes violence?

A. No. He is only the cutting edge. He, too, is
a victim. Responsibility is a seamless garment.
And the northern boundary of that garment is
not the Ohio River.

Q. Are you for desegregation?

A. *Yes.*

Q. When will it come?

A. Not soon.

Q. When?

112

A. When enough people, in a particular place, a particular county or state, cannot live with themselves any more. Or realize they don't have to.

Q. What do you mean, don't have to?

A. When they realize that desegregation is just one small episode in the long effort for justice. It seems to me that that perspective, suddenly seeing the business as little, is a liberating one. It liberates you from yourself.

Q. Then you think it is a moral problem?

A. Yes, but no moral problem gets solved abstractly. It has to be solved in a context for possible solution.

Q. Can contexts be changed?

A. Sure. We might even try to change them the right way.

Q. Aren't you concerned about possible racial amalgamation?

A. I don't even think about it. We have to deal with the problem our historical moment proposes, the burden of our time. We all live with a thousand unsolved problems of justice all the

113

time. We don't even recognize a lot of them. We have to deal only with those which the moment proposes to us. Anyway, we can't legislate for posterity. All we can do for posterity is to try to plug along in a way to make them think we—the old folks—did the best we could for justice, as we could understand it.

Q. Are you a gradualist on the matter of segregation?

A. If by gradualist you mean a person who would create delay for the sake of delay, then no. If by gradualist you mean a person who thinks it will take time, not time as such, but time for an educational process, preferably a calculated one, then yes. I mean a process of mutual education for whites and blacks. And part of this education should be in the actual beginning of the process of desegregation. It's a silly question, anyway, to ask if somebody is a gradualist. Gradualism is all you'll get. History, like nature, knows no jumps. Except the jump backward, maybe.

114

Q. Has the South any contribution to make to the national life?

A. It has made its share. It may again.

Q. How?

A. If the South is really able to face up to itself and its situation, it may achieve identity, moral identity. Then in a country where moral identity is hard to come by, the South, because it has had to deal concretely with a moral problem, may offer some leadership. And we need any we can get. If we are to break out of the national rhythm, the rhythm between complacency and panic.

This is, of course, an interview with myself.

ROBERT PENN WARREN was born in Guthrie, Kentucky, in 1905. He entered Vanderbilt University at the age of sixteen to study for a scientific career, but found the study of literature more interesting. Having graduated *summa cum laude,* he went to the University of California for his master's degree, then to Yale University, and in 1928 to Oxford as a Rhodes scholar.

Upon returning to the United States, Mr. Warren turned to teaching—first at Southwestern College, then at Vanderbilt University. In 1934 he moved to Louisiana State University, where in addition to his teaching duties, he was one of the founders and editors of *The Southern Review,* one of our most distinguished literary magazines. From 1942 to 1950 he was Professor of English at the University of Minnesota, and in 1944-45 also served as Consultant in Poetry at the Library of Congress. From 1951 through January, 1956, he was a member of the faculty of Yale University.

Although he had already received a number of prizes for his poems, it was not until 1939 that Mr. Warren published his first novel, *Night Rider* (reissued by Random House in 1948), and won his first Guggenheim Fellowship. In 1943 came *At Heaven's Gate,* and in 1946, *All the King's Men,* which won him the Pulitzer

Prize. His fourth novel was *World Enough and Time* (Random House, 1950). *Brother to Dragons: A Tale in Verse and Voices,* appeared in 1953 and his most recent novel, *Band of Angels,* in 1955. Mr. Warren has also published three volumes of poetry and a short-story collection, *The Circus in the Attic,* in addition to many critical studies and textbooks.